Paths, Walls and Steps/Volume One

Collins Step-by-Step Guides

Paths, Walls and Steps

Volume One
by Adrienne and Peter Oldale

Collins/Glasgow and London

Printed in Great Britain by
C. Tinling & Co. Ltd.
London and Prescot

SBN 00 435440 0

Contents

Contents (continued)

Good tools do not guarantee good work, but they do make life more pleasant. The main ones, other than the usual spade, rake and wheelbarrow, are shown here.

Tool Kit

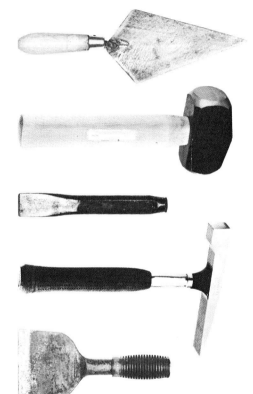

Trowel: these come in various sizes, for cement work. There are rectangular types, called floats, for levelling and smoothing concrete.

Club hammer: $2\frac{1}{2}$lb. head, short hickory handle, for breaking up stone and for using with chisels.

Chisel: for stone and concrete cutting.

Bricklayer's hammer: square-headed, chisel-backed, for trimming stone and brick.

Bolster: a broad, sharp chisel for easy cutting of slabs and bricks.

Builder's level: as long as possible, with both horizontal and vertical glasses; and a straight-edge can be useful, also.

Some tools, especially machines, are hired. These include cement mixers, usually petrol, but sometimes electric powered, and vibratory rollers. The latter are vital for tarred limestone work on drives, and are always useful for all kinds of asphalting.

Random-squared stone paving, laid on soil
and with plants growing in the joints. One of
the loveliest—and most expensive—of
garden path materials.

Introduction

Paths, walls, drives and steps are the most
expensive items in building a garden today.
A small area of stone paving would probably
cost more than all the plants, shrubs, trees,
seeds and fertilizers for the garden put
together. In sheer *effort* too, 'solid' work calls
for more than most garden jobs, and the
materials for a path may well weigh several
tons.

Yet paths and walls do more to improve
the appearance of a garden than most other
features. They give it shape, create a pleasing
design from a bare stretch of land, provide
support for slopes and make pleasant
walkways. A good path, well proportioned
and soundly laid, can vastly improve an
otherwise dull plot. Equally, a harsh-coloured,
crude, roughly-built one can destroy any
chance of making an appealing garden.

The materials and methods used must be
selected with care, so that the results blend
with the character of the garden. In a
cottage-style, 'Old-English' design, a soft
brick path, or one of random stone, would
look better than brightly coloured concrete
slabs. Yet such colour can be very effective in
gardens of modern, functionally laid out
houses.

Most gardeners tackling a new plot will
have a general idea of the style of garden
they want to achieve. This may be quietly
formal, with neatly arranged, regularly
patterned beds, or irregularly charming, with
meandering paths leading to hidden
backwaters; or perhaps, an open sweeping
style of broad lawn, boldly curving paths,
with a few choice, carefully placed shrubs
and trees.

Taste in gardening is individual, and no
two people would plan the same design on
the same plot. Nor does this book set out to
show which sort of path, which wall
material, *ought* to be selected.

What will be found here is simple, direct
information about all the main types, with
their pros and cons set out, their
comparative costs (in money, time and
labour), the methods best used for speed,
strength and simplicity, and a gallery of
pictures showing the work being done.

In fact, this book is hardly meant to be read
at all! It is more in the nature of a tool, a
handy reference guide, or a simple
dictionary of the craft of garden 'hardware'
building.

Above all, it is a book for using, a book to
carry with you outdoors, as you plan the
work; a book to prop on a slab while you lay
paving; to tuck into a pocket while you lay
out a new wall; to keep handy when you go
to order materials.

Nobody would claim that any reader of
this book would be transformed overnight
into a master mason, or could then go out
and teach a bricklayer his job. As often as not,
there are two or three different ways in which
a particular job might be tackled. All we have
done is to show those methods, the simpler
the better, that will work. Given a little care
and patience any man—or woman too, in
most cases—should be able to produce
sound, attractive work with the minimum of
fuss and effort.

Section One

Paths Drives & Patios

There is no basic difference between a garden path, a drive for a car, or a patio, except strength. The same materials may be used concrete, gravel, asphalt, and so on, and the methods of construction are almost exactly alike. The difference will lie in the thickness of the surfacing materials, and in the depth of the foundations. For this reason, there are no special sections on Drives or Patios in this book.

Similarly, the making of patios or terraces is basically similar to paths, with only minor points of layout being different—for example, patios built against a house wall must slope away from the house.

Any special points, on making surfaces to carry a car, or laying out patios, are given with the path-making instructions for each material.

A path is simply a place to walk, where the surface is solid and dry. Natural pathways over the hills and forests of the wild are made by the tread of feet, human or animal, often for centuries. Their constant impact gradually crushes the soil solid, and kills off most plants. Building a new path follows the same basic plan: to remove the plants and make solid, strong foundations.

Most garden path materials are intended as a kind of surface skin—asphalt, gravel, stone or concrete—over a foundation that is already hard. Surfacing materials laid directly on soil will soon sag and shift, with resulting humps, hollows and cracks.

The first and most important job, then, is to get the path foundations really well prepared.

Fortunately, most new gardens are

Foundation strength depends basically on such materials as old brick rubble, shattered and rammed down.

well-supplied with the ideal materials for foundation work—broken bricks and stones, which builders usually leave scattered liberally around. Sometimes, a layer of topsoil has been crudely bulldozed over them, and they are found only when digging is started.

Stones of all sizes may be found during digging, while in case of need, it is easy enough to buy a suitable foundation material. Demolition brick rubble is often very cheap, and some quarries sell crushed stone at moderate prices.

The surface materials are of many kinds, and often here the choice is strongly influenced by cost. Gravel is cheap in many districts (it may cost only a few shillings per square yard), while at the other extreme, sawn, random-squared York stone paving, thought by many garden designers to be the loveliest of all path materials, might cost several pounds per square yard. Between these extremes lies the usual range of concrete slabs, in various colours and shapes, solid concrete and asphalt. In paths not subject to heavy wear, there is a choice of less common materials, weathered brick, cobbles or even logs embedded in bitumen.

The greatest caution must be exercised before deciding on solid concrete (concrete, that is, poured wet, directly into place). Such decks are beautifully solid, impervious, wear indefinitely, are not over-expensive and are quite simple to make. On the other hand, they are almost impossible to shift.

Few gardens are completed at one fell swoop and then left undisturbed, unaltered, for ever. Circumstances change. A garage may be added, or a house extension that alters the position of a door and so calls for a change in the path arrangement. Or quite simply, one's own taste may change— making essential some alteration in the layout—more or less lawn; narrower or wider flower-beds; a new rock garden or a greenhouse.

If at this time there is a solid, cast-concrete path to remove, then there is a great deal of

work ahead. And, of course, the better that path was made, the harder it will be to take up.

In new gardens, then, it will often pay to choose less indestructible methods—slabs, perhaps, laid on sand; or a simple gravel path, or even asphalt. All these are relatively easy to alter later, if the need arises.

Planning the arrangement of paths and walls should be done before any gardening work starts.

Then, the soil which must be dug out for foundations can be used to fill in hollows, or make the basis of a rockery, or of a raised terrace. The quantity of soil obtained may be surprisingly large. For example, a path 30 yds. long and 3 ft. wide, needs a foundation

Deep foundations are essential for long-lasting paths, drives and patios. Save the soil for flower beds.

trench about 6 ins. deep. This means taking out about five cubic yards of soil, enough to build quite a large bank. Indeed, it is a good lorry-load, will weigh five tons or so, and the job will not be done over a week-end.

Naturally, not all paths will be built as strongly as this, at first. A few concrete slabs laid on the surface below the clothes-line will do for a start. But the foundation is the heart of a good path, and to lay expensive materials over a poor, shallow foundation is a waste of money and effort. The result will never be sound, will frequently crack, become weedy, and call for constant maintenance.

Few of us realise just how much the apparently solid earth moves, heaves and sinks in our gardens. Clay soils will expand

and contract very markedly (so much so, that there are special rules about building foundations in such conditions). On lighter land, the soil structure may be so weak that settlement soon changes a level but ill-founded path into a bumpy, unsightly row of tilted slabs.

Careful planning beforehand will often reduce the work to be done in foundation digging. The real labour is in wheelbarrowing, carrying the dug soil into its new home. If you can plan a use for this soil beside the path, in the form of a raised bed, a slope, or a rockery bank, half the work is saved at a stroke. An hour with pencil and paper is better than a week with a shovel.

Although the exact run of pathways,

Classic English dignity with large slabs.

There are several specialised shapes in precast wall blocks and paving. These are by Noelite Ltd.

whether straight and direct, meandering, purposeful or decorative, is a matter for individual taste, there are important practical points to consider. For example, it is difficult to make paths that curve in materials such as concrete slabs, or in squared stone. Only very gentle curves can be made easily with bricks. But it is simple to make any shape at all in gravel, asphalt, crazy paving or solid cast concrete.

If the path is to slope, then gravel should be avoided, and bricks would be too slippery. Rough-finish concrete or concrete slabs will serve, while asphalt is a good, fairly non-slip surface. Where there are quite steep slopes, always provide a hand-rail.

Steps are the real answer for a hillside garden, but even here, some means of getting about on slopes instead of steps will be helpful where wheelbarrows or lawnmowers have to pass.

Many garden paths are too narrow. Broad walkways add dignity and are much more comfortable to use, so planning should allow for this. It is much easier to make an existing path longer than to make it wider. You can add a few yards to the end without the joint being detectable. In most cases, though, adding a foot to the width is difficult to do, without the addition being painfully obvious. Gravel is easiest, simply calling for a shift of the kerbing. Bricks, too, may be added fairly readily. But slab paths, that have been in place some years, will be weathered in colour and new slabs added will stand out unpleasantly. Stone, too, will show the difference between old and new. Asphalt is easy to widen, by shifting the kerbs, but the whole surface must be re-covered if the extension is to be unobtrusive.

Consequently, try to plan new paths to their maximum completed width, even if this means postponing, because of cost or time, the completion of their full length.

Before making final decisions on paths or terraces, always make enquiries locally about available materials. Gravel, for example, may be cheap because there is a river working

near by, while stone may be expensive because it has to come from quarries many miles away. Concrete slabs vary a good deal in price from district to district. There are many small, local firms making quite good slabs, that they may be willing to supply direct. Often, a much lower price may be quoted if the stuff can be collected, perhaps in a borrowed van.

At least one nationally known supplier, though, has so organised retail distribution, that his normal prices may be below those of the lowest local maker.

It pays to collect all information, leaflets, price lists and so on. After all, few path materials cost less than about 20s. a yard, all in, so even a small saving per yard is welcome.

For the smaller modern home, a sun-patio in textured and coloured concrete slabs.

Another important, but often neglected, source of supply is to be found in demolition contractors. Wherever road works or major building projects are under way, there will be old houses being torn down, footpaths bulldozed or buried, ancient stone or brick walls flattened. Much of this stuff is sold off willingly, on the spot, by the demolition firm, who may supply at times for the bare cost of transport. These are valuable friends to cultivate if you plan large paths, walls and terraces. Brick rubble for foundations is supplied, too, and occasionally given free by the lorry load.

Local authorities, too, are constantly rebuilding and altering roads, and frequently have supplies of broken slabs, very well suited to crazy paving or the building of block walls.

In hilly districts there are often old, almost or completely disused quarries, where the stone type or quality is not now commercially profitable. If the owners agree, ideal supplies often can be found in such places. Take care, though, not to try your hand at direct quarrying on the stone cliff face. Collect instead some of the strewn-about pieces left over from the last blasting.

In many of these cases, it is necessary to collect the stuff personally. The weight of stone or concrete is considerable. Roughly, a square yard of paving may weigh two hundredweights. (Cast, coloured slabs often weigh rather less.) Half a ton of stone *looks* quite a small heap. Do not be tempted then, to load a ton into a five hundredweight van.

When the rough outline of the garden plan is becoming clearer in your mind, buy a ball of white string and peg out the whole layout on the site. This is easier for most people than attempting to draw and visualise scale plans on paper. Anything in the garden, whether path, terrace, pergola, fence or greenhouse, has a knack of looking much smaller, or differently shaped, than it does in a plan. We all know when house foundations are dug how tiny the rooms appear. With

paths and patios you can get a better impression of the finished plot by looking at the actual size, pegged-out areas.

Often, too, this exercise points out odd facts that would not otherwise be noticed— how the ground falls away gently to one side, or has a perceptible hollow in the garden centre, or how a terrace, placed in one corner, would be totally shielded from all sun by a tree next door. It is easier to shift pegged strings than to re-lay ten tons of concrete.

To sum up: plan your path and patio layout with an eye to disposing of the foundation soil, to future alterations (especially to path width), to the slope of the land and the locally available materials. Then peg out your design, altering and playing with the marker strings till you have achieved a good plan. Then, and not before, you are ready to go ahead with the job.

1 Making paths of cast concrete

The strongest of all garden path, drive, or wall materials, cast concrete is of special use wherever a strong, permanent deck is essential. Perfect as a drive, it may be laid as a garage floor also, or beneath a shed.

In principle, the work is simple enough, entailing making a wooden mould (or shuttering) to support the wet material, which is then poured into place, worked down well with shovel, ramming boards and trowels and then left to set.

After four days in moderately warm weather, or a week in colder conditions, the shuttering is removed, the concrete having then set sufficiently to support its own weight and retain its shape. Concrete is not fully mature for several weeks, its strength gradually increasing as the days pass. For this reason, newly-laid concrete decks should not be given heavy wear for a month, no

matter how well set they may appear.

Although this setting process is often referred to as 'drying', in fact it is not a simple action of this kind. Setting can take place under water. The action is chemical, and complex, involving the reaction of the cement with moisture.

The basic ingredients of concrete are cement, sand and gravel (often termed 'aggregate') in various proportions. The cement coats the particles of aggregate, then reacts with added water to form a solid, interlocked mass. The greater the proportion of cement, the tougher this bonding action is. For garden work, various 'recipes' may be used, depending on the purpose of the concrete, and a list of the usual ones is given on page 96.

Since cement is by far the most expensive of the materials, it is natural to use the lowest

Broad areas of wet concrete are more easily beaten down to level by improvising a large, two-man beating board.

proportion of this, consistent with giving a mixture strong enough to take the projected wear.

The commonest cause of weakness in amateur concrete work is certainly bad mixing, often aggravated by the use of too much water. Perfect concrete is mixed dry, till every part is thoroughly even in texture. Then, water is added gradually to give a mix that is just on the dry side, moist enough to cling together in a ball when squeezed in the hand, but not so wet as to let much water be squeezed out.

Some weakness may be caused, too, by failure to pack the mixture tightly within its shuttering, so leaving air spaces within the body of the concrete. Only relatively small amounts should be shovelled into place, and worked down before more is added.

Concrete expands like metal in hot weather, and may crack; so where large unbroken lengths or areas of solid concrete are required, expansion joints must be provided. These are simply planks of soft wood, embedded in the deck, and dividing it into sections. These sections then may expand freely, but in so doing they merely compress the wood in the joints.

One can buy timbers specially made for expansion joints, ready soaked in preservative, but it is often simpler to buy lengths of thick, soft wood-chip board, and soak these in creosote at home. Whatever is used, the joint must extend for the full depth of the concrete, completely separating each section from its neighbours.

Home casting of large concrete paths is not light work, and too much should not be attempted at one time. (There is a natural tendency to skimp the mixing of the later batches, as one's muscles become weary.) Expansion joints can help here, by forming natural breaks that can be completed, then the adjoining sections can be added later.

If a really large job is to be done, such as a broad drive, perhaps with a garage floor at one end, then one can buy 'Ready-Mixed' concrete, delivered by lorry, ready to pour. There is generally a minimum amount that one can buy, and with small quantities the cost per cubic yard is likely to be high. Certainly, though, much labour in mixing is saved.

If concrete is purchased like this, though,

it is important that sufficient manpower (or womanpower!) be on hand to lay the stuff as soon as it arrives. There are few more horrifying sights than a huge heap of rapidly hardening 'Ready-Mix' piled in one's front garden! Not only men are needed, but tools, too, wheelbarrows, shovels, strong rakes and battering boards. And, of course, the shuttering must have been placed exactly beforehand, so that no time is wasted before spreading the wet mix swiftly into place.

Some companies will add to their load a chemical that will retard the setting process somewhat, a useful factor if assistance is short on the day. One disadvantage may well be that deliveries are not to be had at weekends.   Another method is to hire a small power cement mixer, in which small batches can be mixed easily and spread at once. These little machines are excellent at the job, and can be hired near most large towns, but may work out expensive if the job has to be spread over a week or two.

In general, if you have unlimited time, at intervals such as weekends, and are not in a great hurry to finish the job, then hand mixing will serve. If you can spare a few successive days, then a power mixer will enable you to do the job single handed, with less backache. But if speed is vital and time limited, 'Ready-Mix' is the answer, and as many hands to help you as can be persuaded to join in.

TOOLS
For cast concreting you will need a shovel for mixing and working the materials; a supply of raw timber, planks and short posts to serve as shuttering, nails, a hammer, a spirit level, and a strong rake. To break up foundation rubble a club hammer is useful, while for top finishing and final smoothing you will need a fairly large builder's trowel.

SUPPLIERS
Cement, sand and gravel are bought from builders' merchants, cement manufacturers, and direct from quarry owners and river gravel producers. Cement is of standard price, but aggregates will vary, especially by distance of carriage. Buy locally and in as large loads as possible. Builders' merchants will supply small amounts, at rather high prices, but producers rarely deal in less than a lorry load, often six or eight tons.

Some suppliers will provide 'All-in Ballast', a prepared mixture of sand and gravel. This needs only the addition of cement and water to make good concrete. By using more or less cement, the strength may be adjusted to suit the hard wear of a front drive or the lighter traffic of a rear garden path.

Ready-Mix is bought by the cubic yard, again with a minimum load.

ORDERING
Concrete is sold and made, both by weight and by volume. When ordering, then, you must first know how much concrete you need altogether. This is worked out by multiplying the length, breadth and thickness of the deck together. Since, in general, paths and drives are made roughly 2, 3 or 4 ins. thick, according to wear, the table on page 96 gives the amount of cement, sand and gravel to order.

1 Wooden planks (shuttering) must support the edges of the concrete till it sets. Drive in support posts at intervals.
2 Lay the planks against these posts.
3 Nail the planks in place firmly. Flexible planks require closely-spaced support posts.
4 The upper edges of the planks must be exactly at the finished level of the path. Check that they are level with each other.

1

3

2

4

5 Large stones and broken bricks make good foundations. Arrange them in an even layer.
6 Ram them together with a baulk of heavy timber.
7 Shovel a first layer of concrete over the rubble. 'Chop' it with the spade to settle it down well.

8 Use a short batten held level to beat the wet surface roughly flat. Do not smooth it off.
9 Too rapid drying weakens concrete. In hot weather, cover it with damp sacks or matting for four days.
10 Frost is a danger in winter. Avoid working if it is likely, and protect against night frosts

5

7

6

8

with a double layer of polythene or sacking.
11 The final topping is of finer, perhaps coloured, concrete.
12 Lay the batten across the shuttering boards and beat the surface level with them. Draw off any surplus. Complete the work in short sections and insert expansion boards in long

paths or wide patios.
13 If the battened finish is too rough, smooth it partially by patting with a trowel. Dead smooth surfaces are slippery. Do not over-trowel or the surface may become powdery. After four or five days the shuttering can be removed.

9

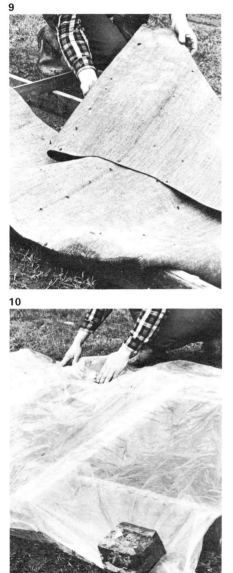

10

11

12

13

2 Making paths of stone inlaid into concrete

This is probably the finest type of paving possible for a garden, combining the strength of concrete with the beauty of natural stone, textured slabs or other surfacing materials.

It is, in fact, a simple development from the plain cast concrete path, and the principle is easy to grasp. Into the surface of the still wet concrete is pushed a patterning of the chosen material. The downward pressure causes wet cement to flow up between the pieces, so locking these into place.

Besides stone and cast slabs, other materials can be embedded—pebbles, cobblestones, even chips of other stones, slates, broken quarry tiles etc.—to make more or less complex textures and patterns.

The concrete for inlay work like this is not brought right up to the top of the shuttering, but rather below, to allow for the volume of the stone pressed into the surface. This may be, say, 2 in. thick, so the base concrete surface must be rather less than this amount below the top of the shutter. If it is too low, the finished level will be low. If the concrete is too high, it will overflow the shuttering when the surfacing material is pressed into place.

Properly done, this method leaves a finish with flat joints needing no pointing and a perfectly flush surface. Only the edge of the path will need tidying, after the shuttering is removed a week later.

TOOLS

The same as for the cast concrete path, with the useful addition, perhaps, of a builder's hammer whose chisel back can serve to trim the surfacing stones to any desired shape; and a small trowel for final smoothing of the joints.

Stone inlaid in concrete will wear almost indefinitely and will never need weeding.

Pebbles embedded in cement make a pleasant change in a large area of plain slabbing.

SUPPLIERS
Sandstone is beautiful for this kind of inlay work, but any sort of stone that is delivered in reasonably flat pieces will serve. Many rocks are in differing shades of yellow or orange, some with coloured veining, while even slate can be used, preferably in combination with lighter coloured stone, to give strong patterning effects. Close and exact fit of the surface stones need not be aimed at, but sometimes an improvement can be made by using coloured cement in the base concrete, so that the joints are not simply dull grey.

Usual suppliers are quarries, who deliver direct, but only in fairly large amounts. Some builders' merchants and many garden centres will supply small quantities, though naturally at a much higher price.

ORDERING
Stone paving can be bought by weight but the area covered by each ton will vary widely, depending on the average thickness and the density of the rock. Only the supplier can give a really accurate guide to this. For inlaying in concrete, stone can be much thinner than for other work (for the concrete below gives the strength), but such thin material may shatter on handling into rather small pieces. Minimum thickness should be about an inch. Paving slabs are bought, of course, by area.

1 Inlay work is exactly the same as solid cast concreting, but the upper concrete layer is not brought right up to the shuttering tops, and may be a concrete made without any gravel. Check each stone for approximate fit.
2 Scoop out a rough hollow in the wet concrete.

3 Press the stone in place and bed it down with light blows from the hammer butt.
4 Lay a batten across the shuttering to check the surface for level and flatness.

1

3

2

4

5 Concrete squeezing up between the stones is worked over with a trowel to embed the stone edges firmly.
6 After the concrete has partially dried, a light brushing will smooth over the joints. Since natural stone may not fit closely, use a sand-coloured concrete so that the broad joints do not look obtrusive.

7 After several days the shuttering is removed.
8 Smooth the rough path edges with fine cement.

5

7

6

8

3 Making paths of concrete slabs laid on sand

Concrete slabs are probably the most widely used of all garden paving materials. Simple to handle and lay, they are now made in differing textures, many colours and various shapes. They are made by casting concrete in moulds, often being strongly vibrated in the process, to make a solid 'set'. The hard grey pavings used in streets are hydraulically pressed, giving a greater weight and strength sufficient for use on drives.

Layout is simple enough, provided care has been taken to get the foundation well prepared and levelled beforehand. Sand is the usual bed on which slabs are laid, each being simply pressed down, then tapped level and butted up to its neighbours.

Cement need not be used in the joints (though if desired, these can be cemented, using the methods shown in the next section on cemented slab paving). Instead, sand is brushed down all the joints, to fill them, yet allow surface water to percolate away.

Well-laid slabs on sand rarely move much, even after some years, yet they are very easy to alter, if need arises, by being lifted and re-laid elsewhere.

Certainly, for amateur use, sand-laid slabs are the easiest concrete paving to lay, and the one that least shows any slight defects.

TOOLS
Spade and rake, a club hammer (or even a length of thick timber) and a level are the only essentials. Where slabs need cutting, as in terraces, or paths with curved edges, then a chisel or two will be needed.

SUPPLIERS
Slabs are sold by builders' merchants, at garden centres, or are delivered direct by

1 Over foundations of rammed rubble, spread a 2-in. layer of sharp sand. Rake it roughly level.

2 Place the builder's level on a six-foot board to check the final levelling. Paving near house walls should slope slightly outwards. Its upper surface must be below the house damp-proof course. Narrow paths can be laid level, the surface water draining through the joints.

1

2

manufacturers. Local enquiries will soon trace the most economical source. The bedding sand must be bought locally, for transport is its heaviest cost. Small quantities are cheapest if collected in a van.

ORDERING

Slabs are sold by the piece to different measurements, the relative sizes being so arranged that they will all match comfortably to each other. 18 in. × 18 in. for example, and a pair of 9 in. × 18 in. will fit nicely together, as will 27 in. × 18 in. All are multiples of 9 in.

Avoid really big slabs (taking 27 in. × 18 in. as the largest convenient size), because they are very heavy, and look crude in small paths. On the other hand, keep the small sizes, such as 9 in. × 9 in. away from path edges, where they are likely to give way easily.

If slabs of differing sizes are to be ordered, make a plan on squared paper, to scale, and determine the exact numbers, colours and sizes that are needed. Order early, if direct from the makers, to allow for delivery delays. Also, be prepared to carry the slabs off the street. Some lorry drivers simply

dump them there and leave the rest to you.

For bedding, use fine ash (often to be had from power-stations), or the rather cleaner, builder's grit sand. Note that sand for this work is rather harsh and coarse, different from the soft, often red sand used for brickwork mortar.

The quantity needed to make a bed 2 in. thick will be roughly 1 cwt. for every square yard. One ton, therefore, will cover an area of about 15 sq. yds.

To make a more permanent bedding, a 'dry mix' of sand and cement is sometimes used, in which a bag of cement is evenly mixed with each six or seven hundredweights of sand. No water is added. The resulting mix is used exactly as plain sand, and brushed down into the joints in the same way. The final watering, to 'settle' the joints, also provides moisture for the hardening of the mix.

3 Lower the slabs gently. Freshly made ones are quite easy to crack.
4 The long nose of a bricklayer's hammer is ideal for driving the bedding sand tightly under the slab edges. Kneel on the slab while working.

5 Never strike slabs with a hammer head. Use the butt, or interpose a piece of timber. Check levels frequently.
6 Minor slab trimming can be done with the back of the hammer. (For more details on cutting, see section on METHODS.)

3

5

4

6

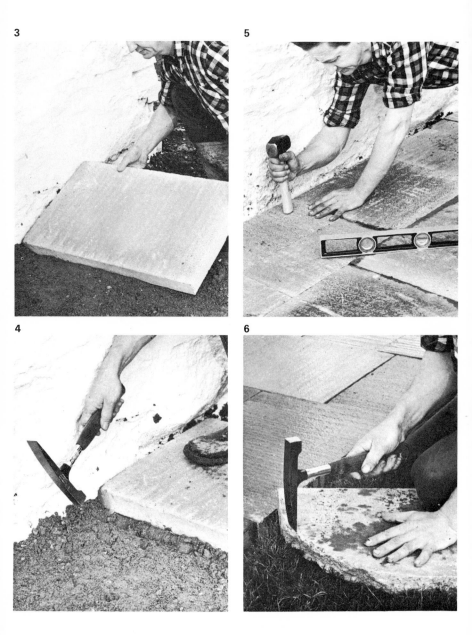

7 Spread fine sand over the completed surface.
8 Brush it out well into all the joints.

9 Water the paving generously to wash the sand in. Re-sand and re-water till all the joints are completely filled.

7

9

8

4 Making paths of soil-based planted paving

Garden paths with small plants growing between the paving stones have a delightful charm, and are easy to lay. They also, however, need a good deal of maintenance later.

Since such paths would not normally be made where traffic was heavy, they can be laid directly on the natural soil surface. If this is to be done, all weed growth must be removed, roots and all, before the job is started. The simplest method of doing this is to soak the whole path area thoroughly with a strong solution of total weedkiller such as Sodium Chlorate. Several such treatments should be given, so that the liquid is forced well down into the soil.

This method has the disadvantage that for six months afterwards plants will not grow in the treated soil, but the complete killing of all weeds is worth the short delay, especially if the weed growth is heavy and includes strong, perennial species with deep roots.

Sodium Chlorate is highly inflammable, and no lights of any kind must be allowed near it, or to the empty sacks or buckets used to contain it. Keep it well away from children.

There are other, more modern types of total plant killers, based on organic chemicals, that act in different ways, and which are sold under trade names. These are not normally inflammable, but are based on very powerful poisons. Some of them may persist for years in the treated soil. On the whole, we dislike this type of chemical, as so many similar introductions, made over the past years, have later proved to be more or less poisonous. Chlorate, apart from its inflammability, seems safe to handle.

Although the soil can be used as the sole foundation for a planted path, there is no

1 Crazy paving is laid on soil, then more fine soil tipped on the surface.

2 Brush this soil into all the joints. Planting can be done as the work progresses.

doubt that a shallow foundation of rammed broken stones gives greater permanence to the path. In many cases, this layer in no way hinders the growth of plants, and may even assist, by improving the drainage near the roots.

Foundations of 3 in. of broken stones, well rammed into a trench of about 6 in. deep, topped with 1 in. of fine, weed free soil to act as a bed and with the surface stones laid in this, will make an attractive and hard wearing pathway. Random-squared York stone is beautiful laid like this, but is very expensive indeed.

TOOLS
Apart from the usual spade and rake, none is needed.

A spirit level is useful, but since such paths need not be geometrically perfect, this need not be bought specially.

SUPPLIERS
Sandstone or other, flat-bedded rock is bought direct from quarries, or through garden centres. Avoid supplies with a large proportion of small pieces, as these are difficult to lay soundly.

ORDERING
Since the weight of stone varies a good deal, only the supplier can advise the weight required to cover a particular area. Old stone flags, expensive but lovely, are sometimes sold by local Authorities.

5 Making cemented, broken-slab paving

Broken paving slabs, often sold off by local Councils at quite low prices, can form the basis of good and permanent paths, having the strength of hydraulically pressed slabs, without the square, bulky appearance of whole ones. (Stone crazy paving can be laid similarly, but because of its variable thickness, it is not easy to make a good solid job.)

The pieces of slab are fitted together on a 2 in. bed of sand or fine ash, like a jigsaw. Then, each piece is bedded at its edge in a fine cement, which is also used to fill the spaces of the joints. A deck like this, if properly made on a foundation of 6 in. of broken brick rubble, will even bear the weight of a car. It is about the cheapest form of the solid types of paving.

TOOLS
Spade, rake, hammer and spirit level are desirable, also a small builder's trowel.

SUPPLIERS
Broken paving slabs are most cheaply bought direct from local Councils, but some builders' merchants and garden centres also supply them. Stone is best bought direct from quarries.

ORDERING
Purchase of broken slabs is by the ton, which will usually cover about 10 sq. yds. Coverage of stone per ton varies with its density and average thickness.

Sand for bedding from builders' merchants will be needed, about half a ton for each ton of slabs. Also, sand and cement for the mortar beds will use roughly two bags of cement and six hundredweight of sand for every 10 sq. yds. This amount, though, will vary with the width of the joints left between the pieces. Coloured cement can be attractive in some cases.

1 Rake out a 2-in. sand bed, then carefully sort out the pieces. Place the larger ones at the edges, to give strength, then fill between with smaller pieces.
2 Work section by section, lifting each piece in turn and placing a generous bed of mortar under its edges only.

3 Lower the piece into place.
4 Tap it down on to its cement bed, which will squeeze partially up the joints.
5 Finally, fill the joints in the top and smooth them over, checking surface level.

1

3

4

2

5

6 Making paths of bricks

The harder sorts of brick, such as 'engineering bricks' are so strong that they wear very well as paving, whereas other types, especially the rough-faced decorative bricks, may flake away fairly quickly. The most usual kind to use, though, are second-hand bricks that have been used on outer walls. These will have been subject to weathering for many years already, so are less likely to flake. They should not be laid flat, as a rule, but stood on edge, which exposes to the air the strongest face.

Although brick drives *can* be made successfully, much will depend on the depth and strength of the foundations. In general, bricks are not suitable for drives.

Path foundations need not be as strong as is necessary with flat, slab-like surfacings. The depth of bricks on edge is great enough to give good strength, if they are laid on sand in a shallow trench, the bottom of which has been well rammed.

A good use for bricks is in combination with other materials, such as concrete slabs, to break the rather harsh texture of these. They also serve well if a narrow slab path is to be widened.

TOOLS
Spade and rake only are necessary, with a bricklayer's hammer a useful luxury for trimming bricks to length in some patterns.

1 Lay one kerb first, setting all the bricks on to a cement bed and drawing more cement up both sides. Let this set thoroughly.

2 Place the bricks to pattern on a 2-in. sand or 'dry-mix' bed, leaving gaps of about $\frac{3}{8}$-in. between them.
3 Bed them firmly with blows from the hammer butt. Check the level.

1

2

3

SUPPLIERS
Second-hand bricks are often bought direct from demolition contractors. Contact with these may be established through builders' merchants, from whom new bricks, if desired, can be ordered.

Delivery will be by lorry, usually to the roadside, so be prepared to carry the supply into the garden.

ORDERING
New bricks are sold by number, old bricks by number or weight. (The number in a ton varies with the type offered.)

4 Now lay the second kerb, also in cement, being generous with this on the outer face.
5 Scatter sand over the surface. Brush this into the joints, using water and more sand as with sand-based paving, till all the joints are filled up.

6 Herring-bone pattern is pleasing. Fill gaps near kerbs with cement.
7 Mixed patterns are fun to make and add variety to the appearance.

7 Making paths of asphalt

Asphalt for home use is sold in sealed bags, and is spread cold. There are several different colours now available, and the finish can be altered by embedding decorative stone chips in the surface. This top coating is laid very thinly, and takes the direct wear of traffic, but its strength depends on the foundations beneath. If these are weak, and sink, then the surface asphalt will crack and sink also.

Full foundations, then, of rammed, broken bricks and stones, topped off with a layer of smaller stones or sharp gravel, are essential. It is good practice, when preparing asphalt path and drives, to do this preparatory work several weeks in advance, letting the normal traffic crush the surface solid. Any hollows that appear are filled in carefully, till a sound, flat and hard surface is achieved. Then, the asphalt can be spread thinly, to seal the surface and give a long-lasting result.

Better still is to buy a supply of tarred stone chips, which are raked out over the foundation rubble and rolled down solidly. This gives the ideal underlay for the fine, coloured asphalt surfacing, but of course, adds a good deal to the expense. Really heavy rolling is vital for this underlay, though the surfacing asphalt can be laid with a light garden roller.

An often unconsidered cost is that of the kerbings, which are essential at path edges, to hold the asphalt in place. They may be of wood (well treated against rot) or cast concrete. Not uncommonly, these kerbs may cost more than the surfacing. If available cheaply, old bricks embedded in cement make a solid and attractive kerb.

These are tarred stone chips, the ideal
foundation for asphalt surfacing.

TOOLS
Rake and roller are vital, with perhaps a spade
or shovel to spread the material. Where tarred
stone underlay is being put down, a really
heavy, power-driven roller can be hired by
the day in most towns.

SUPPLIERS
Surfacing coloured asphalt in bags is stocked
by some hardware stores, builders'
merchants and garden centres. Some makers
also supply direct. Decorative chips are often
included free with the bag.
   Black fine asphalt can be bought in bulk,
at a lower price, from local producers, whose
addresses are obtainable from most builders.
   Bulk delivery is in tipper lorries, to the
roadside, and not usually at weekends.

ORDERING
Purchase is by weight, or by the bag, the
different makers usually setting out the
spreading power on the package. It is best to
err on the generous side. It is hard to spread
very thin layers, and small hollows may
absorb quite a lot. Some dealers will allow
extra to be taken away and any surplus
returned. This is a good scheme, for small
areas left uncovered may be hard to fill in
undetectably later.
   Tarred stone underlay is bought by weight,
the covering capacity depending on the chip
size. The suppliers will advise if they are told
the area to be covered.

1 For home use, cold asphalt is sold in sealed bags, ready to lay. Simply tip it out over the prepared, crushed-stone foundations. **2** Rake the asphalt level, about $\frac{3}{4}$-in. deep and then roll it flat with an ordinary garden roller. Warming the rake helps in cold weather. It is often easier to lay a first coat, rolling it roughly level, then to finish with a very thin top coat. **3** Decorative stone chips can be sprinkled over the completed surface and lightly rolled in.

1

3

2

8 Making paths of gravel

The simplest of all path material to lay (you simply tip it on and rake it flat), gravel depends for its wear strength entirely on its foundations. These should be several inches deep, made of broken stones and brick rubble, well rammed. Ideally, this rubble is then 'blinded' with coarsish gravel, again rolled or rammed and then the final, $\frac{1}{2}$–1 in. topping of really fine, clean gravel is laid down. Some gravels contain fine material, and partially set like concrete if laid very wet. They are termed 'self-setting'.

Support at the sides is vital, or the gravel will soon spread everywhere. Concrete kerbing is expensive, so wood strips, painted or creosoted, are often used instead. These must be strongly fixed to short posts.

Some gardeners deluge their foundations with cheap salt, the idea being to discourage weed growth, but nowadays a twice-yearly rake over and weedkiller spray is more usual.

If the foundations are at least 6 in. deep, gravel drives are quite strong enough for cars.

TOOLS
Club hammer and saw (for the wooden kerbing), shovel and rake. A roller is useful, and essential for the 'self-setting' gravels.

SUPPLIERS
Gravel is a wide term, and may mean crushed rocks, sieved out by machine to various sizes, or it may mean pebbles from beaches or river beds. Shingle has a large proportion of rounded pebbles, and does not make so solid a path as crushed stones, which have sharp edges that jam tightly to each other.

Supplies come through builders' merchants, or direct from the manufacturers. Many areas have local gravel pits or stone-crushing plants.

ORDERING
Gravel is sold by weight or by cubic yard and producers will usually supply by the lorry load only, minimum about five tons. Coverage per ton varies considerably with the average size of particle, roughly 10 sq. yds., 2 in. deep being a fair average.

1 Tip a thick layer of coarser gravel over the path foundations.

2 Rake flat, roll or tread firm, then repeat the process, preferably with a rather finer gravel, to give a smoother top surface. All supporting timber kerbs, except perhaps cedar, oak or teak, need a rot-preventive painting.

1

2

9 Kerbing for gravel and asphalt paths

Kerbing accounts for a large part of the cost of many paths in gravel or asphalt. It may be of brick, concrete or wood. It is usually installed before the paths are completed.

1 For concrete kerbs, spread a generous layer of fresh concrete along the edges of the foundations.

2 Press the kerbs down level into the concrete. Jointing cement is not usually necessary, but can be used if preferred.

3 Draw a strong fillet of cement up the inside face of the kerbs.

4 If access is difficult to the outer face, use a short stick to ram concrete between the kerb and the edge of the foundation trench. Allow the work to set well before completing the path.

5 Kerb bricks are similarly laid. Gaps between will allow surface water to drain from the path.

3

1

2

4

5

1 Permanent wooden kerbing is best supported on wooden posts, specially shaped, made from timber 4 in. × 1 in. × 24 in. long.
2 Coat all posts with preservative.
3 Drive the posts in at an angle away from the path. Use a mallet, not a hammer, or wood may split. Driven in like this, the posts resist any outward pressure as the path surface wears.
4 The shape used gives a vertical edge at the top to which the kerbing planks themselves (also painted with preservative) are nailed or screwed.

1

3

2

4

Section Two

Garden Walls

Garden walls are of two main kinds—those built with regularly shaped, man-made materials such as bricks or concrete blocks, and those built of natural materials such as rock.

Certainly, for amateur work, the even sizes and flat faces of cast blocks make them much easier to use. Few natural stones are completely flat on both sides, and this makes accurate building much more troublesome.

Though bricks have been used a great deal in the past, their place has been largely taken over by moulded concrete blocks. These now come in many colours, textures, sizes and shapes. Some, like the familiar screen blocks, combine the strength of walls with a lightness of appearance that is most attractive in modern gardens.

Building garden walls is a simple and pleasant occupation, since it can be done as slowly as desired and, when finished, the result can be indistinguishable from the best professional work.

The most common error is probably that of getting the blocks out of line and not level; two defects that can be averted easily with a ball of string and a cheap builder's type spirit level.

Natural stonework is much more difficult, though the general approach is the same, and the most satisfactory home building in this material is probably 'dry walling' in which no cement is used. It is then easy to correct mistakes.

Brick, which is reasonably cheap, needs careful design in garden work and some practice in laying to get good effects. Often it is best used in combination with concrete blocks or natural stone, especially the random-sized rubble wall, in which smooth clean corners and cappings are hard to achieve.

Solid cast concrete is rarely seen, except for retaining walls holding back steep banks, but this work should be left to professional builders. The penalty for a collapsing retaining wall may be much greater than if a low, decorative garden wall should fail.

Few jobs are so satisfying as building, and with modern materials there is no reason why any man or woman should not build strong, permanent structures of attractive and professional appearance.

It is difficult to produce good flat wall tops and pillars from non-dressed stone alone. Using brick in combination with stone rubble solves this problem neatly.

10 Making walls of bricks, blocks and dressed stone

Walls built with concrete blocks are justly popular, for these are nowadays made in many sizes, textures and colours, and their regular shape makes them exceptionally easy to erect. Moreover, a little practice with blocks enables brickwork to be tackled too, for the methods are virtually the same.

The two principal ways of building with blocks are to have them all of one thickness, or of different, but related thicknesses. Many walls, especially those that are fairly low, look well if built up of several rows, or courses, of blocks only 2 in. thick. Others are arranged with blocks whose thicknesses are designed to blend with each other (as illustrated). In these, some may be 2 in., some 4 in., and others 6 in. thick. Thus, a double row of 2 in. blocks may be laid level with a single, 4 in. block, and so on.

Natural stone is dealt with in the same

general way, the rock being first sorted into pieces of roughly equal thickness. These are then built up, in regular or varied courses. Since stone is rarely found precisely flat and regular in shape, it follows that the courses are less regular than in cast blocks, and so more difficult to keep level. One can buy dressed stone, cut to size, but the price is prohibitively high. Fortunately, there are many concrete blocks whose general appearance is little different from natural stone. These are often offered as 'reconstructed stone'.

There is (or should be) a limit of height to which amateur wall building is done. Four feet is ample. Tall walls are difficult to erect strongly enough to be permanently reliable, and call for the building-in of buttresses or piers at intervals.

Walls holding back soil should be built no more than 3 ft. high, and only after some

1 Though most garden walls do not require such deep foundations as those of houses, it pays to take out a trench at least 9 ins. deep and several inches wider than the blocks or bricks being used. Ram the bottom firm.
2 Spread a substantial layer (4 ins. minimum) of concrete over the whole bottom of the trench.

practice in the work. Pictures and notes about this problem are given on page 60.

Often, amateur work is spoiled by lack of care in mixing the mortar used to hold the blocks or stones together. This is frequently made too wet, resulting in a weakening of the cement's adhesion, and a tendency to release water which runs from the joints and over the wall face.

Mortar, usually of 1–3 cement to fine sand in proportions, must be really well mixed, not too much at a time, and used within half an hour. After this time, the cement will have started to set, and will have less gripping power.

TOOLS
A builder's level, with a vertical glass, is essential; string and a small trowel also, and a spade for foundation work.

SUPPLIERS
Blocks are stocked by builders' merchants and garden centres, or are delivered direct by the makers. Stone is best bought direct. Dressed stone is so dear that quarries will often deliver even small quantities to local addresses. Bricks are usually ordered through builders' merchants.

ORDERING
Blocks are sold by number, but the makers will usually be glad to quote by the 'yard super', which is the quantity of block required to build a wall 1 yd. long and 1 yd. tall. Normal blocks have only one textured face, but special ones with moulded ends (for wall corners and ends) or double faced, can be ordered. Half sizes, too, are cast, for making vertical endings. Only the 2 in. thick type can be cut easily.

Undressed stone is sold by the ton (the quarry will quote the average building yardage for its own product), but dressed squared stone is sold by the yard super. Bricks are always sold by number.

1

2

3 Consolidate the concrete by ramming it with a baulk of timber.
4 Make the concrete level. If this is truly laid, later building is made much easier.

5 Let the foundation concrete set, then spread a layer of cement, nearly as wide as the blocks and 4 ft. long. 'Joggle' the cement down the middle with the trowel-tip.
6 Lay a similar cement bed at the other end of the wall and lay the first blocks, one at each end.

3

5

4

6

7 Shift the guide string, that has been used to outline the trench, to a point just above the outer edges of the two blocks.
8 Bed each of these down into the cement.

9 Apply a little cement to the end of another block . . .
10 . . . and place it against the first, lining it up below the string guide.

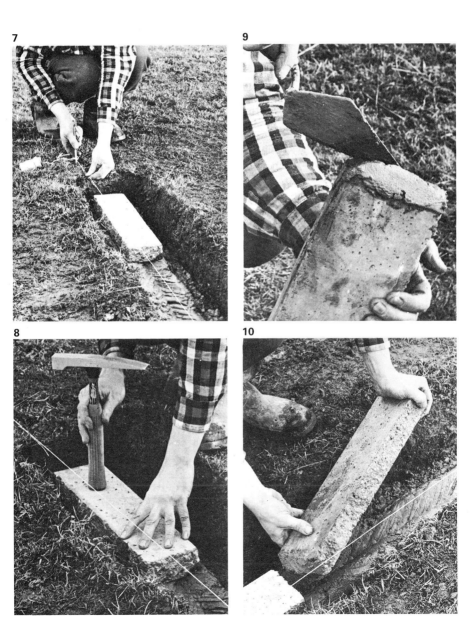

11 Add more blocks, at each end of the wall, till they are above ground level.
12 Now, trap the guide string below a loose block so that it runs exactly along the upper edges of the blocks at each end of the wall.
13 This string now gives rapid guidance to building further, but keep checking with the level at times.

14 Check also for vertical. When both ends have been built up a few courses the space between can also be filled. In this way, the ends will be truly vertical, where it most shows, and the courses there serve as supports for the string guides as filling in is done. Also, any necessary cutting will be done near the middle of the wall, where it is least noticeable.

11

13

12

14

11 Making a screen block wall

Screen block walling is a comparatively modern development, and many patterns are now made, in different colours. Although the method of use is similar to 'solid' blockwork, there is greater need for perfect accuracy in levelling and making vertical. Also, as they are commonly used for screening, the blocks must be built up considerably higher than the 4 ft. maximum we recommend for other walls.

Some makers also supply pre-cast interlocking pillars, into which the blocks slide, making the erection of other piers unnecessary.

Although professional builders will run up such screens quite quickly, using no more than ordinary mortar to secure the blocks, a great deal of added strength is given if simple reinforcements are built in. The cost of this is negligible, and adds greatly to the wall's security. The pictures show these methods,

adapted for amateur work.

Children could easily be injured by any collapse of these walls, so the small cost and time taken is surely worth while for the additional security.

TOOLS
As for blocks. A wooden mallet is useful at times.

SUPPLIERS
Builders' merchants, garden centres, or manufacturers.

ORDERING
Sold by numbers. (Halves are made.)

54

Though screen blocks and their pillars can be erected without extra reinforcement, this is nonetheless so easy to give that it should be done, especially where the finished height is to be over 4 ft., and where the wall stands alone, unattached to any house wall.

1 Reinforcement of pillars is done by inserting a thin iron rod (bought from a blacksmith or some builders' merchants) up their hollow centres. Bend over the tip of the rod and press it several inches deep into wet foundation concrete.

2 Carefully level the foundation concrete before starting to build, then let it set well.

3 Drop a trowelful of cement at the base of the pillar reinforcing rod.

1

2

3

4 Lower a block over the rod.
5 Tap the block gently into its cement bed. Check for level, lengthways and crossways.
6 Fill the central hole completely with concrete, pressing it well down and keeping the rod central.

7 Spread cement on the top of the first block, lower another on to it, and continue building.

4

6

5

7

56

8 Many pillar blocks have a slot to receive the screen block edges. It is not necessary to fill this slot with cement: a small amount in each corner is adequate.
9 Lower a block into the corner. It need not bed absolutely against the pillar but should be slid well into the slot.

10 Hand pressure, or light blows with a wooden tool will be sufficient to bed the blocks together. Only a thin layer of cement is needed in the vertical joint.
11 Upper courses may be strengthened by cross-wire reinforcement. First spread a thin layer of cement over a pair of blocks.

8

10

9

11

12 Bend over both ends of an 18-in. length of thick, galvanised fencing wire (from hardware dealers) and press it on to the cement to span the vertical joint beneath.
13 Bury the wire with a second cement layer and bed the next block course in this. Only alternate blocks need be wired in this way.

14 Perfectly vertical building is vital for strength and safety. Check this frequently.
15 Where screen walls adjoin paving, fill any remaining gap with cement.

12

14

13

15

12 Making drystone walls

There is no telling where the 'rock garden' ends and the 'rock wall' begins. A steepish bank in which stones are embedded may blend imperceptibly into a nearly vertical wall in which the soil is used to bed the stones to each other.

Of all decorative garden walls, the 'floral wall' is probably the simplest to build, easiest to alter and most attractive. Many kinds of plant, especially alpines, will grow happily amid the cracks and crevices of the joints, and if the wall top is left open a still wider range of colourful flowers can be grown.

Almost any flat stone—or even broken concrete block—can be used, and no cement is required. Each stone rests on a bed of ordinary fine soil, and is in turn covered with more soil that supports the stones above.

As with all walls, a permanent structure should have a sound foundation, preferably of concrete, but for 'first attempts' a shallow trench of rammed earth will do quite well.

The rules are simple. Use the larger stones mainly at the base of the wall; lean the faces backwards (rather than vertical), and try to make each stone overlap the joint between the two below.

Planting can be done as the wall is built.

TOOLS

Apart from a spade, you can build a 'floral wall' without any special tools. A hammer is useful.

SUPPLIERS

Stone is best bought direct from quarries. Broken slabs are often sold by local Authorities and make quite good walls.

ORDERING

By the ton or yard super. Suppliers will advise requirements.

Stone is best, especially sandstone and some limestones.

Concrete slabs must be well bedded. Their smooth surfaces do not grip the soil so well as those of stone.

1 Though not essential for all dry walls, a foundation made with 3 or 4 ins. of concrete gives extra security.
2 Use the larger stones for the lower courses. Spread 1 in. of fine soil and press down on each stone to bed it firmly. Hammer more soil between and behind the stones. Each one should bridge the vertical joint in the course below.

3 Give each face a pronounced rearward slope. Besides making the wall more secure, this is better for many plants. The stones should also tilt slightly inwards, to carry rainwater into the wall, rather than letting it run down the face.
4 Make the courses as level as reasonably possible, especially the top two. A short board makes a good sighting guide.

1

3

2

4

5 Brush loose surplus soil from the wall face.
6 Planting of the faces may be done as building goes on. Finally, the open top is filled with plants, or it may be capped with solid, large flat stones.

5

6

13 Making retaining walls

1 Walls that hold back soil are under continuous pressure from behind. They should only be built after some experience has been gained with other types. In any case, 4 ft. tall should be the absolute maximum for amateur work.

Drystone walling, if accurately made, can be a beautiful feature in its own right when the plants on it are mature. It is unsuitable for loose, unstable soil types.

2 Where slopes are very large, it is much safer, for technical reasons, to use two or three small walls rather than one huge one. Cemented stone, though expensive, is most attractive for garden use.
3 A fine retaining wall embodying most good features. Solid concrete foundations;

random, cemented rock, provided with drains to release water trapped behind the wall; and a neat, solid coping of brick.
4 At roadsides especially, the clean lines of concrete or cement-rendered brick may be softened by a good hedge planted above. This type is excellently strong and will withstand considerable pressures.

Section Three

Garden Steps

Most gardens are not quite flat; and a slope, no matter how slight, usually means a step or two being built. With skill, care and vision, a flight of steps can be made to add a new dimension of beauty to a simple garden. Most of us, though, have less than this in mind when we build garden steps, the essential things being strength, comfort in use, and ease of construction.

Fortunately, steps of the size and number usually needed are not very difficult to build, even for unskilled hands. Often, the main problem is simply to decide how many, how big, and how steep. There are many flights of steps (even professionally built ones) that have one step a little larger, deeper or shallower than the others, due to some miscalculation at the start. One simple layout method, not involving mathematics or tricky measurements, is shown in the pictures.

Whatever the length or angle of the steps, a very good rule is to make them each of such a size that adding the depth (in inches) of the tread, to *double* the height, totals as near 26 in. as possible. For example, a step 14 in. deep should rise by 6 in.
(14 in. +6 in. +6 in. =26 in.). This gives a step that is comfortable to the average adult.

Materials for steps may be brick, stone or concrete blocks, or any combination of these. The risers may be rows of bricks, with the treads made of concrete slabs or stones, or cast block may be used throughout, as in the pictures.

Steps vary a good deal in the traffic they must bear. In a new garden, it may be adequate to use a simple, soil-bonded design. Where traffic is heavy, cement instead of soil must be used. It will also be essential where step treads are made of several pieces of stone, for the tread must be rock-solid and strong.

Where strength and permanence are of paramount importance, solid cast concrete may be used. Although this type is relatively simple to construct, there is considerable skill needed to make its massive solidity blend with the garden near by.

Avoid both very shallow and very high steps. Five or six inches is best. And do not forget a handrail at the side of steeper flights, always useful for the elderly and vital for all of us when it is icy.

14 Making steps with blocks

Although garden steps can be made of several materials, it is best to start by using thin, cast concrete blocks bedded in soil. This type, while quite capable of taking the usual wear inside a garden, are the easiest to lay out, and to alter later, if need be. Errors in construction are not permanent, as they tend to be with cement-bonded work. Once experience has been gained with this sort, it is not difficult to progress to the more complex and hardwearing kinds.

The layout method shown consists essentially of dividing the slope into equal sections, each representing one step. The number of steps will depend on the length of the slope, and its steepness. Division into sections 18 in. or 20 in. apart should give steps of comfortable size.

No foundations, other than rammed soil, are shown, but for steps carrying a lot of traffic it is best to bed all the stones or slabs in cement 2 in. deep, allowing for this in the excavation. Or better still, make solid concrete steps as shown in the next section, but inlay stone into the treads to give a softer appearance.

Curved and angled stairways, though made similarly, are only for experienced home workers.

TOOLS
Spade, hammer, trowel, string and a good level are essential.

SUPPLIERS
See under Paths and Walls for the materials concerned.

ORDERING
Tread area is calculated and bought in square yards.

Risers in blocks are ordered in yards super (see walls).

1 To lay out steps for ordinary garden use, first skim out the soil to a regular slope.
2 Mark out the slope with pegs into equal sections. About 20 in. between the pegs will give steps of comfortable size.

3 Place pegs at both sides of the slope, exactly level with each other.
4 Run a string from peg to peg.

1

2

3

4

5 Dig backwards level with each cross string, removing the soil.
6 Finally dig downwards to mark the risers of the steps.

7 Start on the flat part at the very bottom of the flight. Lay a slab on a bed of fine soil or sand, and hammer under its edges till it is firm and dead level.
8 Tip more fine soil over the rear part of this slab.

5

7

6

8

9 Lay the risers (which may be slabs, walling blocks or bricks), on the soil and bed them down firmly.
10 When the riser is at a suitable height, fill behind it with soil, and bed another slab on top, letting its outer edge protrude outwards a little way from the riser face.

11 Brush away any surplus soil and add steps till the flight is complete. In all cases, cement used instead of soil will give a stronger job, but the methods remain the same.

9

11

10

15 Making cast-concrete steps

Wet-cast concrete is one of the most versatile materials to use in gardening, since it can be shaped in so many strong and varied forms. Steps are cast quite simply, by erecting wooden boards or shuttering to the desired shape and size of the steps, then pouring the wet mix into place. The treads are levelled carefully but often left rough.

Where strength and durability are of prime importance, this type will outlast all others; and they are not difficult for home gardeners to make. Take considerable care to get your shuttering perfect, with step edges dead level and all the boards solidly fastened together, or the pouring and working may shift them, spoiling the job completely.

If perfectly smooth wood is available, it is possible to get a cleanly finished face straight from the mould, needing only a little neat, dry cement to be brushed into the remaining tiny air-holes. Usually, though, the cast faces are rather rough, and need smoothing off, a job easiest done with a thick cream of cement and water, smoothed on with a broad trowel or float.

Coloured cement such as Colorcrete, gives a greatly improved appearance without extra work.

TOOLS
Spade, level, saw, hammer, a trowel and some timber for shuttering.

SUPPLIERS
See Concrete Paths.

ORDERING
The volume for a solid flight of steps is given approximately by multiplying the length, breadth and depth of each step, and multiplying the result by the number of steps. For example, a flight of four steps, each 6 in. high, 12 in. deep and 3 ft. wide, would require $\frac{1}{2} \times 1 \times 3$ per step $=1\frac{1}{2}$ cubic feet, a total of 6 cubic feet for the whole flight. This allows a little extra for the foundation bed.

1 Dig the slope to an even angle, as for block steps, section 14. Erect shuttering at each side; then nail cross-boards to support the fronts of the steps. All but the lowest of the cross-boards should have a 2-in. space beneath them, and the upper edge level with the lower edge of the one above.
2 Shovel concrete behind every cross-board.

3 Beat the wet concrete flat with a short piece of timber. This gives a roughish finish.
4 For a smoother finish, use a float trowel to pat the wet surface and bring up a 'cream' of cement that can then be smoothed out. After four or five days remove the shuttering and fill the concrete faces with a thick cream of neat cement smoothed on with a trowel.

1

3

2

4

Section Four

Methods & Hints

1 Throw mixture from heap to heap to give an even texture.

2 Concrete is mixed by pouring water from a fine-rosed can over the whole pile and turning it to an even consistency. Cement or mortar have their water added by opening up a 'crater' in the top of the heap and pouring it into this from a bucket.

Building is a very ancient craft, and over the years many specialised methods, time and money-savers, have been discovered. Of all these, though, some are of special importance to the newcomer, such as how to mix concrete, or how to cut slabs to shape. Others are largely money-saving, as the one we give here showing how to cast your own concrete slabs.

As with most jobs, *doing* is the best way of learning. An hour with a trowel and cement is worth a day with a textbook. So these few pages are only aimed at starting you off on the right lines.

Concrete is made of cement, sand and gravel, in various proportions. Mortar is made of cement, sand and sometimes lime, but *without* gravel. Oddly enough, the mixing methods differ slightly.

To mix concrete, pile up the sand and gravel, and tip the cement on top (only mix about 15 or 20 shovelsful altogether). Then, shovel the whole pile to one side. Next, shovel the pile back to its original position. This repeated movement will mix all the ingredients, and make certain that there is no unmixed portion at the centre of the heap. When all is well mixed dry, sprinkle water on the heap from a fine-rosed can, turning the pile till it gradually absorbs it. It is better to make concrete too dry than too wet. A lump squeezed in the hand should hold together and not lose much water.

Mortar is prepared similarly at first, the dry ingredients being mixed thoroughly. Then a crater is opened up in the top of the heap and water poured into this. The shovel is used to work the heap gradually into an even consistency, 'chopping', and finally turning, the heap several times.

16 Casting concrete slabs at home

Home made slabs need a concrete mix of one part cement (coloured if liked) to three parts of sharp sand.

1 Make a few frames of wood, 2 in. × 1 in., to the desired size.

2 Join three corners of the frame with tacked-on strips of leather, webbing or tin.

3 On the fourth corner, nail cord to one side and drive a short, thick screw into the other.

4 Then tie the cord round the screw to draw the pieces together.

5 Place the frame on a flat, solid surface such as a garage concrete floor, or level, hard earth. A sheet of polythene stretched over will protect the surface. Scatter a $\frac{1}{4}$-in. layer of clean sand over the interior of the frame.
6 Smooth this out evenly.
7 Tip the concrete, mixed on the dry side, into the frame.

8 Spread the mix into every corner, 'chopping' it with a spade.
9 Beat the surface flat with a length of wood. This gives an irregular finish, good for garden use, without further effort.

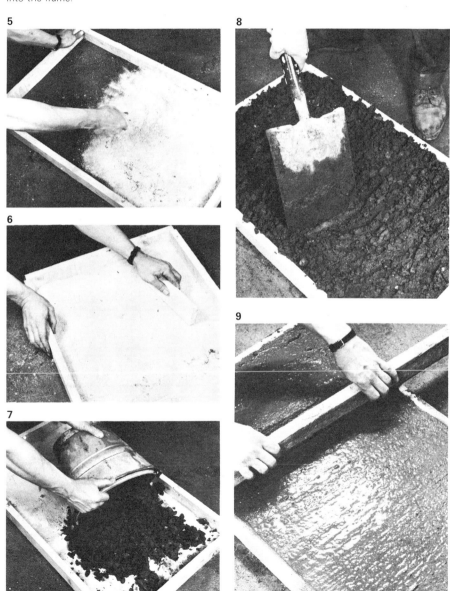

5

6

7

8

9

10 A rectangular float trowel will give a smooth finish if worked over the concrete when this has started to dry, after a few hours. Do this swiftly. Over-trowelling causes the surface to become powdery.
11 Other patterns may be made by outlining the damp cement with a trowel tip.

12 This 'block' effect is easily made by patting the wet face with a float and then opening up 'joints' with its edge.
13 An sttractive and non-skid finish can be made by chopping at the surface with a wooden ruler, to make squares.

10

12

11

13

1 Another simple, non-skid surface is given simply by drawing a brush across the wet cement.
2 After a day or so, the cord can be untied and the frame drawn away outwards.
3 An 'exposed aggregate' finish is attractive and is easily made by including a proportion of gravel in the mix; then, when the slab is partially set after a day or so, scrubbing the surface with plain water.
4 This uncovers the gravel chips embedded in the concrete, making a pleasing, variously coloured texture.
5 Keep newly-cast slabs covered with damp sacks or newspapers to prevent too rapid drying out. They can be lifted up after four days and must be stored on end for a further three weeks to attain their maximum strength.

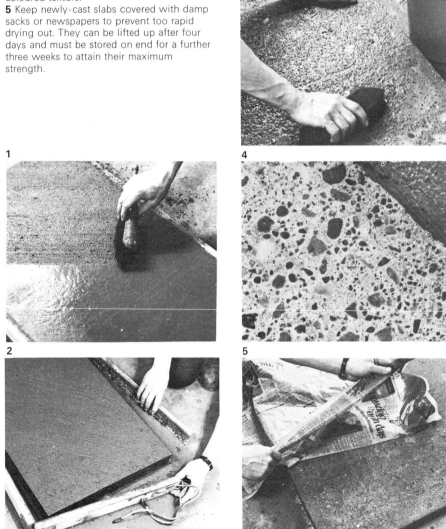

17 Cutting and shaping stone or concrete slabs

Slabs in concrete or of stone are cut and shaped in much the same ways. Cast slabs, being regular in texture and thickness, are easiest at first. Thin stones (less than $1\frac{1}{2}$ ins.), are difficult to cut, for they shatter under the chisel.

1 First, mark the cutting line with a straight edge.

2 Use gentle blows on a chisel to cut a shallow scratch across the slab face.

3 A broad 'bolster' chisel makes it easier to cut a straight line. Then cut a second scratch on the other face of the slab, exactly opposite the first.

2

1

3

4 Cut across the edges similarly, to join the two scratches.
5 Strike the slab face, along the line, firm but not violent blows with the hammer. After some time, the clear, ringing tone of the blows will deaden, indicating that the slab is cracking apart.

6 Most slabs will part reasonably accurately along the line. Any minor irregularities are trimmed off with the chisel.

4

6

5

1 Accurately curved corners are cut by first marking the exact shape on the face of one corner.
2 It is essential that the second cut, on the back of the slab, should be of exactly the same shape. Lay a paper or card sheet over the slab corner and scribble it with a pencil. The outline of the first scratch will appear.

3 Cut the card to the curve.
4 Use it as a pattern in the marking of the back face.
5 Tap the cut face systematically till a portion cracks away.

1

2
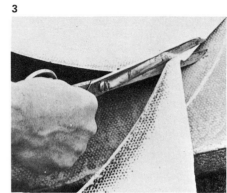

3
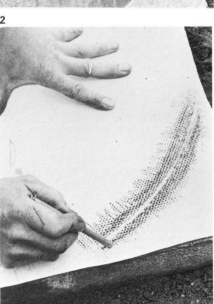

4

5

6 Trim off any remaining irregularities with the chisel.
7 Concave curves are much more difficult. Mark the curve required, but then cut off the whole corner diagonally.

8 Mark a V-notch in the waste part to be removed, and chisel this carefully away.
9 Sharp chisels are essential for this sort of work.
10 Finally use a narrow chisel to remove the concrete back to the curve. As with all cutting, it is best to bed the slabs being cut on a heap of sand or fine soft soil.

6

7

8

9

10

11 Holes are needed sometimes for drains or sunken post holes. Notch the outline with a very narrow chisel.
12 Chip out a 'crater' in the middle of the ring. Do this on both sides of the slab.

13 Finally the chisel point will break through.
14 Careful chipping can now shape the hole to any size.

11

13

12

14

15 Holes of less than 4 ins. diameter must be drilled. Make a large number of holes right through the slab, nearly touching each other, and chisel out the waste carefully.

16 An abrasive disc edge will make the preliminary scratches very swiftly and easily. It is a useful tool when much cutting is to be done. Shield the eyes from grit.

17 Bricks cannot be cut lengthways very easily, but part well across if struck a sharp blow with a broad bolster chisel.

15

17

16

Steps up the middle of a steep drive do not impede cars but make foot traffic much easier.

Section Five

Questions & Answers

For ease in movement, 'walk' heavy slabs from corner to corner.

I have a steeply sloping drive up to my house from the roadside. This is uncomfortably steep to walk on, and dangerous in frost. How may I improve this?
Build a flight of simple steps right up the middle of the drive, so that the car wheels bridge over them.

Can I make a concrete path that can be used at once?
By using high-alumina cement, you can make a mixture that will set hard very quickly indeed, even down to a few minutes. Such rapid hardening weakens the concrete, but this is still strong enough for most garden purposes. See your builders' merchant about the various makes.

I want to make a path of large slabs, but find these difficult to manoeuvre. How can I ease the work?
Big slabs (27 in. × 18 in. or larger) are very heavy. To shift them, when a trolley is not available, 'walk' them from corner to corner. Be very gentle on hard surfaces, though, or corners may crack off.

The garden walls adjoining my garage are of old brick with rather crude repairs in cement and concrete. I have considered using a cement paint over them, to match the white house walls, but the surface is very poor and flaking. What can I do?
Paint over the flaking surface with a bonding agent such as the Blue Circle 'Stabilizing Solution'. This, when dry, prevents powdering and the cement paint can be easily applied on top.

A bed of sand gives a good base to slabs inlaid into a lawn.

I have a slippery green moss forming on my slab paths, which makes walking rather dangerous. How can I get rid of this growth?
This sort of moss, or algae, is usually killed by spraying it with Tar Oil, as used for winter spraying of fruit trees. This can be bought from nurserymen or seedmen.

What is the cheapest garden path?
Probably ordinary, household ash, well watered and rolled down on to a broken rubble foundation. But it is messy. You will need some sort of kerbing, too, to hold the ash in place. This can be creosoted wood, or old bricks well embedded in the soil. A topping of clean gravel now and then makes all the difference, and is not expensive.

Is there any special problem about making a path of slabs, inlaid in a lawn?
No. Simply excavate 1 in. deeper than the slab thickness. Spread a layer of sand over the bottom, and bed each slab in this. The final level should be just below lawn level, to ease mowing.

When is the best time of year to make garden paths?
This depends on the material. Asphalt is best laid in warm, even hot, weather, when the material will remain plastic much longer. Avoid very cold spells. Wet-cast concrete must never be laid in frost, or the resulting path will be very weak. Yet hot weather will cause it to dry out too swiftly. The ideal is a wet, cool, misty period such as we often get in Spring, or in Autumn and early Winter. With slab or brick work, any season will do.

I am laying a new concrete garage floor and have been advised to insert a damp-proof membrane. How do I do this?
Such a membrane is simply a large sheet of thick polythene, sandwiched in the floor concrete. Lay this 2 in. lower than your proposed final level. Smooth and let it set. Spread the sheet, with the edges rising up the wall a few inches. Lay a final 2 in. layer of concrete on top. The sheet edges are best cemented into the joints of the wall, above its damp proof course.

I want to build a wall along one boundary of my garden, but my neighbour claims that the fence is his, and he will not have it altered. Can he prevent me building my wall, if I do it *inside* my boundary?
No. You can build what you like (in reason) within your own land, putting up a wall as well as the existing fence. But remember, you will have to do *all* the work, and the maintenance later, from your own side. You have no right to cross the boundary to build or to make repairs, and if the job is done against your neighbour's wishes, he may later stand on *his* rights too.

A polythene sheet sandwiched into a new
concrete floor is an effective damp-proof
course.

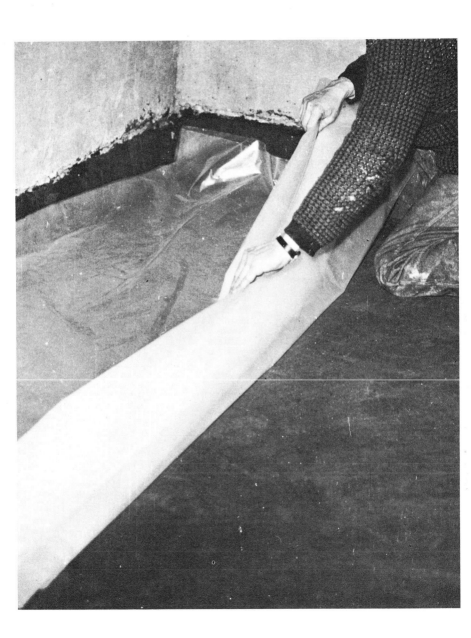

I recently built a new patio at the rear of my house. Now I find that damp is rising up the house wall where it adjoins the patio. Yet the slabs slope away from the house. What has gone wrong?

You have almost certainly buried your house wall damp-course. Water soaking through your patio foundation is getting into the wall above its damp-proof course (DPC), causing rising damp. (You can often find your damp-proof course by carefully studying the brickwork of the wall, looking for a layer of thick felt or asphalt in one of the horizontal cement joints, about 6 in. above the original ground level.)

Rising damp can be wholly cured only by taking the patio away from the wall, and clearing this down to DPC level again. Then re-lay the patio below this level. As very much a second-best, you can apply to the wall, from DPC upwards, several thick coatings of damp-proofing liquid of bitumen base, perhaps with a sheet of DPC felt material sandwiched in the coats. This may do the trick, but it is not good practice save in exceptional cases.

I have no garage or access from the road. Can I build a drive myself, and carry it out over the pavement?

You can do all the work inside your garden boundary, but all work on the footpath or roadside (assuming the road is adopted) must be done by the local council, who will charge you for it. Before starting any such work, do consult the local council surveyor, because any vehicle outlet needs permission. This is not usually refused, except where some danger may arise.

I have a rather sensitive skin. Will cement affect it?

Yes, cement and lime affect most people, if handled when wet. Apply a good barrier cream and wear tough gloves. Wash the hands thoroughly and frequently as the job goes on, if contact with the cement is unavoidable.

What is the simplest and quickest way to resurface an old concrete path?

There is a bitumen-based, self-adhesive sheet with a surface finish exactly like asphalt. This is Temple Pavex and is simply unrolled over the old concrete (after filling in any actual holes with cement). It gives a remarkably long-lasting surface.

What is the best material, expense apart, for a private patio, with a sun-roof overhead?

If the patio is really a kind of outdoor room, reached directly from the house, terrazzo tiles are most luxurious and wear indefinitely. They come in many blends of colours. They are laid like ordinary concrete slabs, on a 2 in. bed of mortar. Do not cement them together, though. Butt them tightly, then flood the surface with a slurry of cement, like cream, which will run into the joints. Clean off the surplus as it dries, and polish it well.

Where the design allows, perfect, sawn sandstone flags are very fine, and are probably the highest in cost of any material.

I have an old, solid concrete drive, the surface of which is now rather poor. Can I re-surface this in any way, without taking it all up?

It is difficult to re-surface a concrete drive with concrete because the new will not adhere to the old. Often, the new surface soon cracks away. By shuttering up the sides and laying on a full, 2 in.-thick layer of well mixed concrete, you can do the job well, but rather expensively.

Another solution is to use asphalt on the surface. First paint the old concrete (after cleaning it well) with a bonding agent bought from any builders' merchant. Then rake out bagged asphalt about $\frac{1}{2}$-in. deep, and roll it down well. At the edges, fit creosoted timber kerbs to hold the asphalt firmly.

A 3 ft. high stone wall that retains the soil at the rear of my house is leaning slightly outwards. It has been like this for some time. How can I strengthen it?

Temple Pavex, a bitumen-based self adhesive sheet path surfacing that is simply unrolled into place.

The best solution, without doubt, is to take the wall down and rebuild it with a slight rearward slope. Since the defect is of long standing, however, it will probably be safe enough to build a buttress or two of cemented stone, leaning up against the wall face, at intervals of 8 ft. or so. Watch these later, though, for tell-tale cement cracks indicating that the wall is shifting further.

I have one garden wall made of large, ugly concrete blocks. I would like to pebble-dash this, to soften its harsh colour. Is this easy?
Pebble-dashing into a cement skin is not very difficult in theory, but calls for practice to get a neat finish. A fine cement coat is wiped on to the wall face, and then the pebbles are flung at it. Those that stick are pressed gently flat with the blade of a plasterer's float. Much easier to use Cullamix Tyrolean finish, which has a similar appearance to fine pebble-dashing. This material, though, is sprayed on by a small, hand-turned machine (that may be hired for only a few shillings wherever the Cullamix is sold). This job is quick and easy, and several different colours are made.

I have frequent visitors to my hillside garden. Would I be liable for damages if they fell and injured themselves?
In general, you *would* be liable, especially where, say, adequate handrails had not been provided, or where steps were slippery with moss. Besides checking these points, you could also take out an addition to your insurance policies to cover you against claims of this kind. The premiums would probably be very low.

A double kerb-wall with plants is most attractive.

Simplest damp-proof course for a brick or block wall is a strip of special bitumen felt sandwiched into a horizontal joint.

I want to grow ivies, and other climbing plants, over a brick wall, but have been told that ivy damages the structure. Is this so?
In general, a thick growth of ivy seems to protect the wall, rather than damage it. But the brickwork must be sound to start with. You cannot easily point the cement after the growth is on it. But why not apply a trellis of wood to the wall face, to which your plants can cling? You can then grow other species, such as clematis, as well as the self-clinging kinds.

I want to build a low, but decorative, boundary between my drive and the front lawn. What do you recommend?
A very low double wall in cemented stone, and filled with soil. Many plants flourish in such conditions. The stones also act as a kerb for the drive surfacing, if desired.

I am building a concrete drive, but the job will take some time, as I am only free at weekends. Should I buy all the materials at once, or bit by bit? I have plenty of storage space and want to save cash if possible.
Buy all the sand and gravel you will need—with a generous allowance for error—at one go, for it is expensive to buy small quantities, and delivery is hard to arrange.
  Cement, though, should not be stored (except indoors in a warm place), even in unopened bags. Damp air can cause it to part-harden in the bag, and even the remainder, apparently unaffected, may in fact set rather poorly. Buy only as much cement as you can use each weekend.

I have a very steep 6 ft. high bank behind my house, of solid clay soil. What type of wall should I build to retain this?
It is dangerous for an amateur to attempt to build tall walls, especially retaining walls. The pressures are enormous. If the bank is sloping at an angle of 45° (one in one), then it is unlikely to slide much for some time. But the only safe advice is to get the job looked at by a surveyor.

I have a supply of old quarry tiles. Can I use these for paths outdoors?
Quarry tiles will stand the weather well, but their surface is very slippery, especially in wet weather, so they are not really desirable. NEVER use them on steps. But you can build charming walls with them, cementing them like bricks, with a cement made 1–3 with builders' sand. Clean off any old polish first.

What is a 'DPC' in a wall?
DPC stands for damp-proof course, and is any waterproof material arranged to act as a barrier to damp. A common kind, easy to instal, is a strip of bitumen felt, sandwiched in a joint, 6 in. above soil level. Always put one in walls supporting buildings.

I have heard of log paths. What are they?
Lengths of logwood, usually 6 in. or 8 in., are soaked in liquid preservative. After drying, their lower halves are coated with bitumen and the logs are then stood upright, touching, on a 3 in. bed of dry sand. More sand and gravel are brushed between and the whole lot hosed over. More gravel is packed in till the logs are held tightly. Such a path will wear a long time and is very soft underfoot. It is not cheap, unless the wood is available locally.

Section Six

Materials Costs Maintenance & Repair

Cast Concrete

Wet-mixed concrete is poured between wooden moulding boards (called shuttering) and left to set. This is the very strongest kind of paving and wears indefinitely. It can be coloured or finished with various patterns and textures; if left plain it is rather harsh-looking for garden use. The cost is fairly high. Self-mixed dry materials are about 10s per sq. yd. 3 in. thick: ready-mixed concrete varies, but is usually 8s to 12s per sq. yd. 3 in. thick in large loads.

Maintenance

Very little. 'Dusting' of a new surface may occur. There are proprietary dust-suppressing fluids.

Repair

Cracks may be chiselled a little wider, especially at the underside of the deck, and filled up with cement mixed 1–4 with sand. If the crack is caused by absence of expansion joints, however, the trouble may recur. If the surface flakes, only fairly thick (min. $1\frac{1}{2}$ in.) resurfacing will do any good. Thin layers flake off again.

Slabs and Stone Inlaid in Concrete

Slabs and stone inlaid in concrete combines the immense strength of solid concrete with the charm of natural stone, textured slabs, pebble-cobbles and other attractive finishes. The surfacing materials are pressed down into a deep layer of wet concrete. It looks superb and will wear indefinitely. But it is expensive, for you will need a minimum 3 in. of cast concrete, plus the surfacing stone. New thin stone might cost anything from 12s to 30s per sq. yd. according to what is available locally.

Maintenance
Very little.

Repair
Occasionally a surfacing stone may work loose. Chisel out its bed about 1 in. deeper, and re-bed the stone in cement mixed 1–4 with sand.

Slabs Laid on Sand

The commonest of modern path materials is slabs laid on sand. Easy to lay, extend and alter, and available in different colours, textures and shapes, its wear strength depends largely on its foundations, which are often rammed brick rubble and sand. Suitable for all foot traffic, but on garage drives only strong, hydraulically pressed slabs can be relied on to take the weight indefinitely, and these are not often made in colours other than grey. Price, however, is moderate; the bedding sand will cost 2s to 4s per sq. yd.; grey slab suitable for drives roughly 15s per sq. yd.; and coloured slabs for garden use from 15s to 25s per sq. yd.

Maintenance
Weeds may spring up in joints and at the edges. Liquid weedkillers, watered on as required, are simple and effective. Beware flooding at the edge, or neighbouring plants may be damaged.

Repair
Some sinking of slabs may occur. These should be lifted clear, a little sand scattered in the low part of their beds, then lowered again. On no account try to hammer down raised corners. Lift them and remove a little of the underlying sand.

Planted Paths Laid on Soil

Strictly for garden use where traffic is light, planted paths laid on soil make the most charming of all types of path or terrace. The joints are of soil and so can be filled with low growing plants, especially those that can tolerate treading. It is relatively cheap to make, provided the stone is available locally; but is unsuitable for cars or loaded wheelbarrows. Apart from the cost of plants, which can obviously vary a great deal, the stone may cost from 12s to over £2 per sq. yd., the thicker and larger pieces costing most. Stones differ in their covering capacity per ton, but your supplier will advise on this. Squared slabs are *very* expensive: the strong and splendid squared York stone is one of the dearest paving materials available.

Maintenance

Continuous, at least during the growing season. Hand weeding is essential. Weedkillers would destroy the plants too.

Repair

Edge stones often tilt. Hammering soil under their edge will usually raise them to level again.

Broken-Slab Paving

Laid on a foundation of raked sand, crazy-paving slabs are solidly jointed with cement to give a clear, weedproof surface. Being relatively cheap, yet without the rather stark appearance of plain grey slabs, this is a popular path material. Its wear strength depends on its foundations, and the care with which it is laid. Although not really suited to motor traffic, it will serve for a few years if need be. Since this is largely second-hand material, cost is usually moderate, ranging around 8s to 10s per sq. yd. To this add the cost of bedding sand at roughly 2s 6d per sq. yd.

Maintenance

A few weeds may get rootholds in cracking joints, but these are easily hand pulled.

Repair

If pointing of the joints should become loose, often after frost, pick out the pieces and refill with fresh cement, well pressed down. This trouble is usually caused by insufficient joint-bedding cement having been used in the first place.

Brick Paths

Another primarily 'garden' material, brick should not normally be used for drives. Although not all kinds of brick wear well (especially sand-faced types), it is of pleasing, cottage style appearance, easily laid and altered. Weeds may become a problem after a time. Brick paths are low in cost; cheap if the bricks collected, and, as they are sometimes given away free, price will depend on negotiation with the demolition contractor, but will probably be around 5s per sq. yd. New bricks would cost from 15s per sq. yd., and true hard 'engineering' bricks from £2 per sq. yd.

Maintenance

Stiff brushing will keep down moss growth. Weeds in joints call for a liquid killer. Kerbing is the most likely source of trouble.

Repair

Broken or sunken bricks can be lifted fairly readily and replaced. Keep the kerb cementing well repaired, especially the outside supporting fillet.

Asphalt and Bitumen Paths

Although many roads are made with 'hot' asphalt, for garden use there is a mixture that is laid out cold, straight from bags. Easy to lay, yet professional in appearance and moderate in price, this is another popular material. Old paths can be renovated with it, too. Strength is completely dependent on good foundations, which are best made with tarred limestone. It is suitable for cars, if properly based. Cost is moderate. Allow about 15s per sq. yd. for a $\frac{3}{4}$ in. surfacing. Cost of underlay tarred limestone etc. varies, but allow roughly the same amount in preliminary calculations.

Maintenance

Occasional trickles of liquid weedkiller along kerb edges. Clear dirt occasionally from angle of kerb.

Repair

Patching is hard to do invisibly. If possible, give a light skimming over the whole surface. Collapse is most usual near edges. Vigorous heating with a flame-gun (these can be hired), may soften newish surfaces sufficiently to allow complete re-raking and rolling, so calling for no new material. If a localised patch sinks, do not remove it. Hammer it down further and fill in above with fresh asphalt.

Gravel Paths

On flat land, gravel serves well, and would be the cheapest of all, but for its need for kerbs to hold it in place. Wood or concrete kerbing will serve, but neither is cheap. Some gravels have a sandy texture and partially set to a weak concrete appearance. Although gravel is easily disturbed, it is equally soon re-raked to a good finish again. On sound foundations a 2-in. layer will cost roughly 3s per sq. yd.

Maintenance

Rake at least twice a year to bring new gravel to the surface. Weeds are a nuisance, so liquid weedkiller is essential, at least annually.

Repair

Check all kerbs for security occasionally. After wear, gravel becomes embedded in the ground. Spread a quantity of new gravel on top.

Blocks, Bricks and Dressed Stone

Concrete blocks make the easiest permanent wall of all for amateur building, strong, quick to erect, in many colours and designs. Bricks are a little harder to deal with, while cemented stone requires a fair amount of skill. The general methods are the same in all cases. Broadly speaking, the larger the blocks the cheaper per yard the wall will be, but really big blocks look ungainly in most gardens. For $4\frac{1}{2}$-in. thick walls, large blocks cost from about 25s per yard super (3 ft. high by 3 ft. long) with small blocks from about 40s per yard. Copings for the top are from 1s 6d per foot. New bricks cost from 35s per 100, there being roughly 50 bricks to each yard super.

Maintenance

Check occasionally with a builder's level to detect leaning or subsidence. Remove weeds rooting in joint cracks.

Repair

Re-pointing may be done if the cement becomes weak or crumbly. Rake out all the joints an inch or so deep and press in a stiff cement mortar. There is a special tool for this, but a squared stick will do. Or the cement may be finished almost flush, with a trowel. Walls that lean or actually collapse should be taken down *completely* and rebuilt from the foundations up.

Screenblocks

Beautiful effects can be achieved easily with decorative screen blocks, which are rapid and simple to build. Accuracy of vertical alignment is essential, and a coping stone across the top must be used to prevent weather damage to the top row. A good block for amateur use, and it is easy to build in reinforcement. It is the only sort to use for walls more than 4 ft. high. The screenblocks themselves cost from 35s per yard super upwards. Pillars are about 7s 6d per foot high, copings from 2s 6d per foot.

Drystone Walling

True 'dry walls' have no bonding material and call for high skill in construction. By using soil as the bond, the work is made much simpler and quicker. Mistakes are easily remedied later. Plants of many kinds will flourish on this wall.

Maintenance

Hand weeding, and a check for loose stones, is all that is required.

Repair

As building.

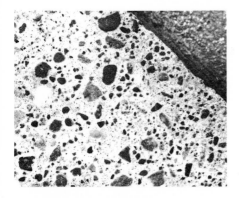

**Materials required for one square yard
of concrete**
For Wall foundations, Drives and Garage
floors:

	Cement	Sand	Gravel
2 in. thick	30 lb.	$\frac{1}{2}$ cwt.	1 cwt.
3 in. ,,	45 lb.	$\frac{3}{4}$ cwt.	$1\frac{1}{2}$ cwt.
4 in. ,,	60 lb.	1 cwt.	2 cwt.

For garden paths, large steps and retaining
walls:

	Cement	Sand	Gravel
2 in. thick	37 lb.	$\frac{1}{2}$ cwt.	1 cwt.
3 in. ,,	55 lb.	$\frac{3}{4}$ cwt.	$1\frac{1}{2}$ cwt.
4 in. ,,	75 lb.	1 cwt.	2 cwt.

For thin paths, small steps, slab casting and
cement mortar:

2 in. thick	56 lb.	$1\frac{1}{2}$ cwt.
3 in. ,,	85 lb.	$2\frac{1}{4}$ cwt.
4 in. ,,	112 lb.	3 cwt.

Note that sand and gravel vary slightly in
weight, but the above will give concrete of
proportions reasonably suited to home use.

If your supplier cannot deliver 'All-in Ballast',
order coarse grit, sand and gravel, in the
proportions 1 part sand to 2 parts of gravel,
to the same *total* volume as the 'All-In'.